ABBÉ JULIO

His Life - His Work - His Doctrine

by

Robert Ambelain

ABBÉ JULIO

His Life - His Work - His Doctrine

by
Robert Ambelain

Translated and introduced by
Tau Phosphoros

TriadPress
Hainesville, IL

Abbé Julio: His life, his work, his doctrine
by Robert Ambelain

Translated and introduced by Tau Phosphoros

First English Edition
Published November 2021

ISBN: 978-0-9973101-2-2

Triad Press, LLC
260 E. Belvidere Rd. #357
Hainesville, IL 60030

Table of Contents

INTRODUCTION

  This short work by bishop Robert Ambelain, in Ecclesia Tau Jean III, is a concise but informative overview of the life and works of bishop metropolitan Julien-Ernest Houssay, better known as Abbé Julio. It seems only fitting that bishop Ambelain would produce this short biography. Ambelain is best known for his work in the Gnostic Church and its affiliated rites. During the second World War, when esoteric orders and societies were being forcibly suppressed throughout Europe by the oppressive Nazi regime, Ambelain was one of the few brave souls in France who helped to ensure the continuity of these movements, which included not only the Gnostic Church, but other bodies of mysticism such as Martinism, the Ancient & Primitive Rite of Memphis-Misraim, the Rose✠Croix d'Orient, the Ordre Kabbalistique de la Rose✠Croix, the Elus Cohen, and others. Some of these orders and societies were preserved only in "seed" form, that is the initiatic spark had been preserved and little more. And it was largely upon Ambelain and his close colleagues to reconstruct many of these bodies from the barest of both secret and published documents.

  Another venerable Patriarch of the Gnosis, Eugène Fabre des Essarts, in ecclesia Tau Synesius, had written another short biography of Abbé Julio decades prior, and which appeared in *Les Grand Secrets Merveilleux*, the first volume of Abbé Julio's 3-volume opus, which includes also *Prières Liturgiques* and *Le Livre Secrets des Grand Exorcismes et Benedictions*, and which have been translated by us and published as *Grand Marvelous Secrets*, *Liturgical Prayers*, and *The Secret Book of Grand Exorcisms and Benedictions*. Tau Synesius was a personal friend and student of Abbé Julio, as well as the Patriarch of the Gnostic Church founded by Jules Doinel (Tau Valentin II). So, we can see, therefore, that Abbé Julio and his works have long been influential with the Churches of the Gnosis. And it has likewise devolved upon us now to make all of these works available to an English-speaking audience.

The information found in Ambelain's essay overlaps slightly with that of Tau Synesius, but complements it on the whole. While it does not give some of the historical data contained in the work of Fabre des Essarts, it supplements it with facts not found elsewhere, including a thoughtful exposition of the philosophical and theological underpinnings of Abbé Julio's work. Most of these speculations are well-grounded in established facts, while in a few areas I think Ambelain's paper reveals more about his own views than those of Abbé Julio. For instance, on the topic of reincarnation, Ambelain staunchly rejects the notion that Abbé Julio accepted this doctrine in the least. He even goes so far as to state that the very doctrine of reincarnation was a 19th century fabrication, which it is demonstrably not. He says of the good Abbé's works, "One would seek vainly indeed a passage of his works where he supports this theory..." But then he immediately goes on to cite a passage of the *Grand Marvelous Secrets* wherein Abbé Julio seems to be suggesting that he is the reincarnation of Jan Hus. He tries to explain this away as being due to the influence of his colleagues. But we could pull another passage from the *Secret Book of Grand Exorcisms* where Abbé Julio is speaking on the concept of purgatory and expiation, and of earth being one of the expiatory hells: "For many, it is a salutary hell, since it purifies and elevates, when one may finally leave it. For many it is the vestibule of another, more fearful purgatory, because one brings there a new burden to expiate, be it through a return here below, or into another world." In this passage, the "burden" referred to sounds very similar to the Eastern concept of karma, and the expiation "through a return here below" can be nothing other than reincarnation. This view would, in fact, be in perfect concert with the Gnostics of old, who held that the soul must pass through the gates of the archons, and that if one did not have the proper "password," that is if one's soul was not sufficiently purified, spiritualized, it would be captured by the cosmic archons and hurled back into the cycle of incarnation. Nevertheless, Ambelain goes on for some amount of space refuting the doctrine. But we must see this more as a refutation of the *desire* to be reincarnated. For reincarnation is not to be seen as a reward, as in some doctrines, but as a failure. Even Ambelain seems to finally acknowledge as much, for in the very last line of the last footnote at the end of that section, we read: "But reincarnation is certainly a law for the non-Christians."…

       In any case, overall Ambelain, for whom we have the utmost love and respect, has provided many fascinating insights into the great thaumaturge. He is also good enough to give us a useful sampling of some of the healing prayers of Abbé Julio at the end of the work. These powerful prayers have been drawn from among all three of Abbé Julio's great tomes. These highly efficacious prayers give but a small taste of the wealth of spiritual resources found in the 3 volumes. But when applied with faith they may produce the most astonishing results.

As you become more familiar with the remarkable life and works of Abbé Julio, we hope that you will see therein not merely a curious relic of an ancient faith, but a living system endowed with powerful spiritual forces and a gateway to the many blessings of God. May this little booklet be one such gateway, and may the emissaries of Light, all the Good Spirits, the Saints and Archangels, and all the other beneficent intermediaries of God be always near you; for they are already there, awaiting your call, ready to aid and assist in the welfare of our fellow men and women, both of body and soul. Apostolic blessing be upon you, and may the peace of the Lord be with you always. So mote it be!

Tau Phosphoros
Patriarch
Apostolic Church of the Pleroma
31 August, 2016
Feast of Holy Theodotus

I. BEGINNINGS

Julien-Ernest Houssay, who would become celebrated under the name of "Abbé Julio," was born March 3, 1844, at Cossé-le-Vivien, in Mayenne, a large village situated some kilometers to the south-west of Laval, and at the boundary of Ille-et-Vilaine.

He was the son of a small masonry contractor, with whom he came several times to demolish churches falling into ruin and to reconstruct them. Later, Abbé Julio would see there an indication of his own mission.

The natal decan, that the old science of the Stars has analyzed in the course of the centuries, is already significant of the mission of the one who will take his place, eventually, among the most representative personalities of its ten degrees:

"In the second aspect of *Pisces*, rises a woman with a beautiful countenance and well adorned. And she signifies the making of requests and intervention for great and noble things…"

Such is its meaning, that Henri-Cornelius Agrippa gives us in his celebrated *Occult Philosophy* (S.L. 1551), thus resuming an old Iranian tradition. We will find there later on our personage and his noble impulses, as well as, in the "woman with a beautiful countenance and well adorned," that *Church* which would become, less than ten years after his death, the official Church of Martinism, and thus gather several thousand faithful around the world.

If we consult the *Thebaic Calendar*, familiar to the practitioners of onomantic astrology, and which was transmitted to us thanks to the erudition of Johannes

Angelus, the author of that most rare early work known under the name of *Strolabium planum in Tabulis uscendens* (S.L. 1488), we see that the thirteenth degree of Pisces (natal degree where the Sun is situated on that day) has for its hieroglyph *"A man and a woman riding horseback slowly."* For the layman, this signifies a perfect conjugal agreement, a shared love, and good accord in the household. For the bishop (which he would later become), this woman is his own church, that mystical church which he weds on the day of his priesthood, and of which he wears the "ring of fidelity" on his finger.

Being unaware of the natal hour, it is not possible for us to study further the celestial augurs of Abbé Julio. But one will observe nevertheless that Jupiter and the Sun, in conjunction with the sign of Pisces, favored his access to the high religious charges.

He was a priest by vocation, and against the wishes of his family, which precludes any error of orientation from birth. And we find him, as he comes out of the seminary, vicar of the parish of Grand-Oisseau, where he will be found, moreover, when war breaks out with Prussia on July 18, 1870.

The Abbé Houssay immediately becomes chaplain of the volunteers assembled by Cathelineau. Without doubt, these pontifical zouaves are all legitimists, and profit from the situation, soon ashamed for raising the white flag. But the Abbé Houssay marched behind it as he had followed the red flag of Garibaldi and his volunteers with red shirts. And this he later related, himself, to his disciple and friend Fabre des Essarts.

On December 3, 1870, at the battle of Toury, he carried upon his back, to the ambulance, an officer of the pontifical zouaves of Cathlineau seriously wounded. Then, without taking rest, he returned to the field of battle, and saved still ten other wounded.

On the night of December 3rd to the 4th, he guided with prudence and success across the dense forest of Orleans, a group of twenty soldiers who, without him, would have infalliby fallen into the hands of the Prussians.

On January 4, 1871, through snow and cold he hastened to rejoin Cathelineau who, cut off from the rest of the French army, was on the verge of being squeezed in the enemy lines, thus saving more than three thousand men from the rigors of a long and painful captivity in Prussia.

On January 8, after the battle of Vibray in the Sarthe, at the north-west of Vendome, Cathelineau asked him to go seek out the wounded that the pontifical zouaves, in retreat, had been obliged to abandon, in the snow and cold. The Abbé Houssay departed alone, without hesitation, and as always on foot. Along the way he fell into the hands of the Prussians, who stopped him as a spy, and prepared to shoot him. For four hours, and according to good international military tradition, he is beaten and insulted copiously by the soldiery of Frédéric-William. Finally, having held strong, the Abbé Houssay is released; he is finally able to reach the field of battle at Vibray, and tend to the wounded, administer to the dying, and see the to burial of the dead.

On January 21, 1871, we find him at Anger, and general Cathelineau expressed himself thus on his subject: "The brave Abbé Houssay fulfilled his mission admirably, brought volunteers with him, collecting information on each. But he had to surmount immense difficulties, and he

3

arrived only after three weeks of fatigue and marches…"

The peace having returned, he is named vicar at Juvigné, then at Javron, two parishes of Mayenne. But his health is gravely compromised by the fatigues of this harsh campaign where he was entirely spent. And in 1875 he will have to be hospitalized at the military hospital of Amélie-lea-Bains, of which he will be the chaplain besides. The pure air of the Pyrenees helping, it left him healed, and in 1878 he will be named vicar of the Saint Joseph church at Paris.

If our Abbé had adapted to a banal life, looking after his own advancement and not occupying himself with the affairs of others, he would have slid by in the peace of days without history in the midst of the Parisian clergy.

It would, in fact, be quite otherwise…

II. THE BATTLE

Unfortunately for him, and fortunately for the Church, the Abbé Houssay is of those who take for themselves the words of the Psalmist: "The zeal for Your House consumes me, Lord…" And before a cascade of scandals that the high diocesan authorities cover with a pious and grieved silence, the Abbé Houssay finds no place for himself. These scandals, which go from sodomy, practiced upon unfortunate orphans of a well-known institution, to the seduction of young domestic servants, while committing fornication with rich devotees, and collecting inheritances, to which is added at the end of the course, simony, these scandals, our Abbé brought to light in resounding brochures.

On February 28, 1885, he is then mentioned disgracefully at the parish of Sainte-Marguerite, having had the impudence to take legal action, for fraud, against two laymen protected by the bishopric. On March 1, 1885, Mgr. Richard, the Archbishop of Paris, summoned him and said this, that the Abbé Julio has related and that his direct disciple, Fabre des Essarts, has painstakingly recollected:

"We do not have any reproach for you during your stay at Paris; your notes are excellent, and we willingly recognize that you are an intelligent and pious priest. But we believe that you will do much more good in a country cure than in the Parisian ministry. We have, therefore, not any uneasiness, and you may choose such diocese that you please. We undertake to obtain for you a good position…"

The Abbé Julio requested to reflect. Having

understood that they wished to hush him up (and at the same time to withdraw him from the spectacle of scandals which had provoked his indiscrete indignation) by isolating him in a country cure, far away from the intrigues in which he took part, the Abbé Julio refused by letter on the following day, March 2, 1885.

Not being able to place him on interdict, after having threatened him, for there was not "canonical cause" justifying such a measure, Mgr. Richard then saw to refuse to him *material access* to the altars of the Saint-Martin church. The Abbé Julio wrote then to the bishopric of Laval, from which he rose at the time of his debut as priest, and they gave him every permission to celebrate the Mass and to reside in Paris.

We add to his credit that before taking up the avenging pen as his Master had taken the lashing whip, the Abbé Houssay had taken the advice of his curé. Horrified, the latter formally advised him against raising such problems. That is to say that when Mgr. Richard, archbishop of Paris, declared a merciless war against him, the Abbé Houssay found himself alone again. And, in the course of 1885, he then resigned, leaving Rome without any regret.

But his brochures would draw upon him the attention of proper and sincere priests. One of the first who joined him was the Abbé Sterlin, former divisionary chaplain of 1870, like him, and former curé of Plainville, in Oise. The Abbé Sterlin had established himself at Nogent-sur-Marne; he had modest revenues at his disposal. He helped the Abbé Houssay to found a little periodical: "La Tribune du Clergé." Another priest had followed the Abbé Houssay, the Abbé Estève de Signoce. It is he who related one day to Paul-Clement Jagot how, in the modest hotel where he lodged after his departure, they had dispatched to him a simple girl who had for her mission to make him become her lover, and to be thus the instrument of his dishonor, by offering her to provide for his needs. He divulged the well-laid trap.

It is in this "Tribune du Clergé" that the Abbé Houssay took, for the first time, the pseudonym of Abbé Julio. The offices were situated at 21, Croix-des-Petits-Champs street, in the same locale where later would be installed the Journal "L'Eclair" by Emile Buré. Abbé Julio had for collaborators all the liberal priests of the era: the Abbé Deramey, professor at Sorbonne, the Abbés Sanvert, Roca, Jovet.

But Abbé Julio, at a certain moment in his life, and precisely in this period, under the influence of certain secular relations, believed it was possible to lead a campaign for the reconciliation of all religions with a common characteristic: the belief in only one God. He forgot then that Christ had given as mission to his Apostles a categorical instruction, and that mission consists rightly to have them leave every other religion in order to have them become Christians:

The one who does not enter by the Door in the Sheep-pen,· but who enters by another side, that one is a thief and brigand..., (John X, 1).

I alone am the Door... And all those who came before me were thieves and brigands...,(John X, 9).

Do not think that I have come to bring peace upon the earth! I am come to bring not peace, but the sword. I am come to put division between the son and his father, between the daughter and her mother, between the daughter-in-law and her mother-in-law...,

(Matthew X, 34-36).

Go throughout the entire world, and preach the gospel to every creature. The one who will believe and will be baptized will be saved; but the one who does not believe will be condemned…,(Matthew XXVIII, 19 & Mark XVI, 15-16).

And so, Abbé Houssay and the Abbé Deramey, and several of their collaborators, separated from each other offended, and this was the end of "La Tribune du Clerge." But this new orientation of the Abbé Julio had led him to new and useful relations. He had notably made the acquaintance of Madame de Morsier, of the Countess d'Adhemar, of Albert Jhouney, of the Abbé Pochon, of the pastor Wagner. And Albert Jhouney, Martinist and Kabbalist, devotee of Gnosticism, who would give in the course of his laborious career a considerable literary and initiatic work, was, with Papus, the one who would, very rapidly, make the Abbé Julio understand the implicit deviation included in this hope. If there is a Messiah, a Savior, his role is at the same time unique and special, and he could absolutely not be put on equal footing with the *illusory and doubtful* gods, and even less with "prophets" purely human in origin.

Moreover, it was precisely these influential relationships, cited above, that eventually permitted Abbé Julio to reconcile, for a moment, with Rome. We will see how and why.

But at the present moment, the Abbé Houssay knew dark days. He published his *Contes Danois* [*Danish Tales*], a work that we have been unable to find, but that Fabre des Essarts assures is "of high quality." This book did not enrich him, and the publisher no more. He then gives lessons on various topics. The bisopric learn of this, and they soon move to ruin him. He then begins as a bookkeeper in a factory, which assures him his daily bread and modest lodging. But in the evening, in his small room in Belleville, under the rooftops, he received senators, deputies, and future ministers, interested by this concept, new and clear, of the Church, a Church which would be freed from the servitude imposed on it for ages by a caste and an ultrareactionary oligarchy.

And it would support itself with those from the birth of a republic which would no longer be anti-religious because of an obligation to be anti-clerical, and by the imperious necessity for a sort of self-defense.

In January 1888, we find him collaborating with the journal "L'Ami de l'Humanite" [The Friend of Humanity] (not to be confused with "Humanity," which Jean Jaurès would found). From 1888 to 1889, he created and animated a little periodical paper: "La Tribune Populaire," organ of religious democracy and the defense of the clergy. Additionally, from 1888 to 1902, fourteen years, he published another periodical: "L'Etincelle" [The Spark] ("Religious and liberal review"), organ of the union of Churches. Later on, this title will be taken (without his permission of course!), by Vladimir Oulianov, called Lenin, for a Russian language revolutionary review, that the socialist expatriates grouped round Lenin would print by hand secretly at Paris.

It is in this review of religious defense that Abbé Julio categorically attacked the atheistic faction of Freemasonry, in September 1902 (number 116). And it is again in this review, as in his diverse correspondences, that one is able to discover his dogmatic orientation; more than in his various books, these latter being more instruments of work. Moreover, we believe it useful to devote a part of his biography to the study of the various interesting points of this doctrine. He emanates indeed, by this very choice of Abbé Julio and by his rallying to the work of the great Origen, a new image of man, such that one may henceforth consider him as the true founder of the contemporary Église Gnostique [Gnostic Church].

It is towards this era (1888) that he encounters Jean Sempé, extraordinary seer, mystical healer, operating by prayer alone. Jean Sempé, who would die on January 9, 1892, at Vincennes, declared readily that he did not have any of his powers at birth, but rather by a transmission, received equally by another old man, in his youth. he contented himself with prayer; He performed prayer, blessed with the water, the salt, the oil, and drove out every evil "in the name of Jesus Christ," whether the sick was in his presence or far away. This gift he transmitted in his turn to Abbé Julio. He revealed that the simple key to put this transmission into action was Prayer; not the simple, banal prayer, the recitation of the most simple types of orisons, but that in which one undertakes to obtain from God a very precise grace, by connecting it to its initial archetype, always included in the Holy-Scriptures.

And Abbé Julio, in his turn, prayed, healed, consoled, with the gifts, the prayers, and the same success as Jean Sempé.

At the bishopric of Paris, they were disturbed by the orientation that the Abbé Julio had taken. The Church had suppressed already for quite some time all the great exorcisms and rituals of healing which, for ages, had been its strength and its glory. The Roman Pontifical barely preserves the Exorcism of Pope Paul V, the one given by

Leo XIII, and a curious exorcism for the day when one cuts his beard for the first time!

And here is a priest broken from Rome, who involved himself with healing, as a consequence of instructions received by a suspect layman, and not only healing, but even exorcism, that is to say to liberate the bewitched, the obsessed, to destroy the spells, to purify the infested places, whereas his bishop had not only not authorized it, but would not even do it himself.

But this bishop, Mgr. Richard (Cardinal Richard), for want of being a great bishop, was an intelligent man. He thought it most wise to compromise. He made an offer to Abbé Julio to submit himself, assuring him then, with absolute pardon for his undisciplined literary works, his re-entry into grace, and an important post. Abbé Julio refused the post, and, in order to show his submission to the Church when it stayed true to its mission, accepted this submission under certain conditions, those relating to his works of exorcism and healing. Mgr. Richard capitulated. He named Abbé Julio curé at a very humble cure, that of Pont-de-Ruan, at the south of Tours, between Monbazon and Azay-le-Rideau. Abbé Julio took advantage of this stay full of calm and peace, in a province pleasant among all others, to meditate upon multiple problems. In this cure, he had found two works which modified his whole spiritual orientation. The first was a very old Roman *Benedictional*, edition of 1665, from which he took all its curious exorcisms, unaware of the modern Church, and integrated them into his various works. We observe on this subject, and it is not the least amusing of the history, that we know several priests and monks who, in face of the disappearance of the *Book of Exorcisms* (which is supposed to be delivered to the ordained at the time of the ceremony of the *Exorcist*, but which is in our day replaced by the simple Roman Ritual), have actually turned to the works of Abbé Julio!

The second book which had upon him a decisive action, was a study upon the work of Origen, doctor, bishop, and martyr (185-254), one of the glories of the church of Alexandria, condemned wrongly as a heretic by the Council of Constantinople, two centuries after his death, rehabilitated in the nineteenth century, and that Leo XIII did not hesitate to consider, in his encyclical "De Providentissimus," as deserving the first place among the doctors of the Church. We will rediscover his particular doctrine in studying later on this new orientation of Abbé Julio. We note here simply that this discovery made of him a theologian more subtle and more informed than the habitual reader of his works generally suspect!

It is during this stay at Pont-de-Ruan, where he lived two years, that Abbé Julio succeeded in healing an unfortunate soul, become mad following an arbitrary internment in an asylum. Later on, having left Touraine, he lived at Fontenay-Sous-Bois, then at Paris, at number 5 of Vernier street, (17th ward), where he succeeded in installing a little chapel since 1901. Curious thing, it will be on this same street that some years later another unusual personage will come to reside, bearing the same first name as our Abbé…

This would be Jean-Julien Champagne, alchemist already well experienced, and the laboratory where he will work will be offered to him by the family of Lesseps. *And Jean-Julien will become celebrated under the name of Fulcanelli*…[1]

It is, moreover, not impossible that the locale be

the same, for it is in 1907 that Champagne came to Vernier street, and it is in 1907 that Abbé Julio published, at Vincennes, his first works.[2] The occult world (Martinists, Gnostics, Kabbalists, alchemists, etc....) constitute a particular universe, full of resonances, where multiple and very tangled relationships sometimes unite the apparently most separated individuals. And the locale of Abbé Julio could have been pointed out to Champagne by common relationships.

In 1903, Abbé Julio left Vernier street to go and live in Vincennes, 170 Fontenay street. One should remember that it was at Vincennes that he had known Jean Sempé.

---

1. Name that certain ones will attempt to take away after his death! We have given in several conferences, with photographic documents and *definitive proofs* to support it, the demonstration that Champagne and Fulcanelli were but one and the same personage. The text of this conference ought to appear at any moment in one of the issues of 1962 of the review "La Tour Saint-Jacques," with highly probative photographs.

2. He lived then at 170, Fontenay street, in a little house with a garden. Today, at that place, is raised a beautiful five-story building, and the surroundings are considerably changed, as one would suspect.

III. THE CONSECRATION

Jesus, having assembled the twelve, gave them strength and power over the demons, with the power to heal the sick..., (Luke, IX, 1).

Then he opened the spirit to them, that they may understand the Scriptures..., (Luke XXIV, 45).

All that you bind upon the Earth will be bound in Heaven, and all that you deliver upon the Earth will be delivered in Heaven..., (Matthew XVIII, 18).

It is when he resided at Fontenay-Sous-Bois, that the Abbé Julio received one day a visit from Mgr. René Vilatte, of whom he would eventually become one of the successors, in the long and time-honored apostolic lineage descended from the Apostle Peter himself. And it is Mgr. Vilatte who had him consecrated bishop by Mgr. Miraglia, his Coadjutor. The solemnity took place on December 4, 1904, in the parish-church of the Old Catholic Rite of Tienger, in the duchy of Bade, with, as consecrating bishop, Mgr. Paolo Miraglia, bishop of the *Église Catholique Independante d'Italie* [Independent Catholic Church of Italy] (analogous to this was the *Église Gallicane* in France). Here assisted as official witnesses (in addition to numerous assistants), Mgrs. Paul Kaminski, Curé of this Old Catholic parish, and Aloysius Blum, president of the Parochial Council.

We note, in passing, that the *Old Catholic Church*, which gathers around the world several million faithful, in Holland, Germany, Switzerland, South Africa, etc., is a great Church. It was constituted, at the end of the Council of Vatican I, in 1869, by the Bishops and Roman theologians who refused to admit the dogma of the infallibility of the Pope, at the request of Pius IX. Certain of those opposing held out, only to be expelled by force. That very night a violent tempest rose up against Rome. In the winds tearing up trees and chimneys, some saw therein a replica of the "breath" that encircled the dwelling of the Apostles, on the day of Pentecost. Others saw there a manifestation of demoniacal rejoicing, Satan being called in the Scripture, the *"Prince of the air,"* (Paul: Ephesians II, 2).

Here, then, is the Abbé Julio become Monisgneur Houssay. And those who knew him then all affirmed that he had changed. Not at all that his desire, his very passion, to see the CHURCH of CHRIST return to its greatness and first purity, was mitigated. Quite the contrary. But having become bishop, his "battle" changed in plan. He elevated the debate unto the level of *Invisible Causes*, perverse sources of degradation. He understood that the Bishop, the Priest, had in fact but one sole direct Adversary, ever the same, the "Prince of this World."

But was this consecration of Abbé Julio valid? In a word, had the Abbé Julio really become a bishop? That is what we are now going to study, and *demonstrate*.

To the eyes of the Roman Catholic Church, to be *licit* and to be valid are quite different things. An Orthodox bishop not "united" with Rome is *illicit*, but *valid*. The same bishop in the Eastern Church called "uniate" (reunited with Rome under Leo XIII), is *licit* and *valid*. It is thus that when, under the same pontificate of Leo XIII, a part of the Eastern Churches (Syrian, Maronite, Chaldean, etc. ...) entered into the Roman bosom, they did not re-ordain their priests and did not reconsecrate their bishops. They were already *valid*, they became *licit*.

In a word, to be valid is to hold the Succession of the Apostles; it is to be able to prove that one dates it back, *without missing a name*, to one of the twelve Apostles. And this is one accountancy painstakingly kept by all the Churches, as one would suspect! It is also to possess the probative documents of this.

To be *illicit*, is, all while being valid, to belong to a Church called "separated" or not united with Rome. To be *licit* is to belong to the Roman Catholic Church, or to an Eastern Church recognizing its authority, its preeminence, and its dogmas.

And it is because the apostolic succession represents the *Powers*, the *Mission*, the *Privileges*, conferred by Christ to the Twelve, and by the Twelve to their successors, the bishops whom they consecrated themselves, *because it is an essential thing for the Universal and Eternal Church*, that Rome, fairly, makes a distinction between *validity* and *licitness*.

Abbé Julio, by his consecration, became therefore an *illicit* Bishop (since consecrated by a Bishop and by a Church separated from Rome), *but nevertheless a valid Bishop*, since his apostolic succession was unattackable. And this is what we are going to demonstrate; not for the Catholic Hierarchy, which is not unaware of it and no longer contests it, but for the public, often badly informed on these things, essential for Christianity.

On the fact that only one Bishop consecrated him, whereas the traditional ceremony calls for three, the *Consecrator* and his two assistants, we read this in the journal "La Documentation Catholique" no. 948, page 689: "It is absolutely beyond doubt, and strictly established by a long practice, that the Bishop, and that, for the validity of this consecration, *one sole Bishop suffices*, who accomplishes therein with the requisite intention, the essential rites." (Cf. Pious XII: "Apostolic Constitutions, -Episcopal consecration" - 11-30-1944.)

One Roman Catholic Prelate, J.M. Spalding, in his *History of the Protestant Reformation*, (New York, 1875, volume II, page 424, note 2), tells us this, as regards validity in general: The consecration having been duly accomplished by Bishops who had without doubt themselves the episcopal character, was, although not canonical and illegal, certainly valid. Thus, the heretical and schismatic Bishops today, unless the Rites of consecration have been, since then, materially altered, are vested of the episcopal character..." (op. cit.).

It is, moreover, to the Roman Catholic Church that one owes the most coherent of these principles of *licitness* and *validity*, as well as their most demonstrative applications.

Rome, indeed, recognizes the validity of the Episcopates of the Orthodox, Lutheran, Old Catholic, and Liberal Catholic (this is the Church of the theosophical Society).

Thus, then, two conditions are necessary and *essential* to the validity of an episcopal consecration:

1) The consecration must attach the consecrated to the apostolic lineage. The consecrator must therefore be, and validly, a Bishop himself; that is to say, and through the intermediary of his predecessors, to hold his powers from one of the twelve Apostles of Christ. In short, *he must possess the apostolic filiation in order to be able to transmit it.*

2) The Ritual, the material form into which the sacramental grace inserts itself, must be traditional; that is to say that it must convey the will to transmit, on the one part, and the will to receive, on the other part, what constitutes the Episcopate according to Christ.

We mean by episcopate, the function that the primitive Church has transmitted to us, and to which are attached certain *prerogatives* and certain *powers*: power to celebrated the mass, power to remit sins (power called "keys"), power to confer the various sacraments, power, *for the Bishop*, to *transmit* in his turn these different powers, whereas the Priest only puts them into action.

In this Ritual, which varies with the Churches according to whether they are Eastern or Latin, there are essential elements. These last are what constitute the *traditional form* to which the greatest allusion is made.

We now see, therefore, the "links" which, *along nineteen hundred years*, attach the Abbé Julio to the twelve Apostles, and, not a trifling thing, to *Saint Peter himself*.

Mgr. Paolo Miraglia, who consecrated Abbé Julio, was ordained priest in the bosom of the Roman Catholic Church. He even became there "prelate of His Holiness," honorific dignity.

He was consecrated Bishop on May 6, 1900, in the church of Piacenza (Italy), by Mgr. René Vilatte, then Exarch of the Metropolitan Church of America.

Who was Mgr. Vilatte?

René Vilatte had been ordained to the Minor and Major Orders by Mgr. Herzog, Old Catholic Bishop of Berne (Switzerland). He had been ordained successively Cleric, Porter, Lector, Exorcist, Acolyte, Sub-deacon, Deacon, and Presbyter, on June 5, 6, and 7, 1885. These ordinations had taken place according to the Old Catholic Ritual, very close to the Roman Pontifical. The regularity of the Old Catholic episcopate, and of Mgr. Herzog in particular, has never been placed in doubt. The apostolic succession of this last goes back indeed to Bossuet, and from Bossuet to one of the Twelve!

Seven years later the Abbé Vilatte was consecrated Bishop, under the name of *Timotheus*, on May 25, 1892, in the cathedral church of Our Lady of the Good Death, at Colombo (isle of Ceylon). The Jacobite Patriarch of Antioch had sent his authorization (we possess a copy of this in our dossiers); the consecrating bishop was Mgr. Antoine-François-Xavier Alvarez (Julius I), Syrian archbishop of Ceylon, assisted by Mar Athanasius and Mar Gregorius.

Although this ceremony was carried out in the bosom of the *Syrian Jacobite Church*, it occurred according to the forms of the Roman Catholic Rite, at the request of Mgr. Vilatte. The Charter of Consecration of Mgr. Vilatte, that we give further on, was signed, not only by the consecrating Bishops, but even by the Consul of the United States, Mgr. Vilatte being an American citizen then, and having over there an important parish. As regards the apostolic succession of the Patriarchal See of Antioch, from which Mgr. Alvarez held his episcopate, it has never been debated any more than that of the *Old Catholic Church*.

His filiation goes back indeed (we give it in extenso hereafter), *and that without interruption*, to Evodus, first bishop of the great Church of Antioch, which long possessed the primacy among the nascent Church, before being dispossessed of it by that of Alexandria. Evodus had been consecrated by Peter himself.[3]

According to the traditional chronology of the Church, reproduced by Lemaistre de Sacy (1613-1684), writer, historian, and Catholic theologian (he later became a Jansenist): "The year 38 of the vulgar era, and in the year II of the reign of Emperor Caligula, *Peter went to Antioch and there established his see.* In the year II of Emperor Claudius, he went to Lydde and healed Enée..." This is found likewise in the *Ecclesiastical History* by Eusebius, bishop of Cesarea (265-340). The *Grand Dictionnarie de Theologie Dogmatique* also confirms this fact.

So Peter remained a year at most in Antioch, and it is then in 39 (some say 40) of our era, that he consecrated, before his departure, Evodus who is his first successor. It is interesting to note that if Rome had not had more importance (considered as capital of the Empire) than Antioch, out-of-the-way in the East Mediterranean, one would not speak of the primacy of Rome, and the Catholics would not consider Saint Linus as the successor of Peter! It would be Evodus, the first pope after him.

Here, then, the apostolic source of Mgr. Vilatte is well established. It remains to us to give the text of his

---

3. Three *patriarchates* exist at Antioch: The *Latin Patriarchate*, which is Roman Catholic; the *Orthodox Patriarchate*; the *Jacobite Patriarchate*, which directs the *Syrian Jacobite Church*, gathering the *monophysites*. Its patriarch resided formerly at the monastery of Sophar, it is now at Antioch itself. This church gathered before the war close to 60,000 families, in Asia Minor. The *monophysites* (advocates of the unique nature of Jesus Christ) were secretly protected by Empress Theodora, when they were persecuted by the *Melchites*, protected by Emperor Justinian, her husband. And it is indeed in the dungeons of Byzance, that this Church was born, which has innumerable martyrs.

Charter of Consecration:

"In the name of the Eternal, existing in Himself, God All-Powerful, Amen, ✠ Antoine-François-Xavier JULIUS I, by the grace of God, Archbishop of CEYLON, GOA and India, to all those who will read these presents, salvation, peace, and benediction in Jesus Christ, our Lord. We make known to all by the present letters that on May 25, 1892, in the cathedral of O.L. of Good Death at HULDEDORF, COLOMBO, with the assistance of MAR PAUL ATHANASIUS, Bishop of Kottayam, MAR GREORIUS, Bishop of NIRANAM, MALABAR (India) and in the presence of a great multitude of Christians of our jurisdiction and others, by virtue of the powers conferred to us by the apostolic succession and by the favor of H.H. PETER III, Patriarch of the Orthodox See of ANTIOCH, after having invoked by prayer the vivifying Holy Spirit, we have imposed our hands upon Joseph-René VILATTE, Parisian by birth, American by naturalization; we have consecrated him with the holy oils for the archepiscopal dignity, following the forms of the Latin Rite, under the title of Archbishop of the Ancient Church of America, and we have confided to him the power to ordain monks and priests, to consecrate the Churches, the altars, the cemeteries, etc…, etc…, to perform all the functions belonging to the rank of Metropolitan.

Given in our archepiscopal residence, Cathedral of O.L. of Good Death, COLOMBO (CEYLON) today, feast of Pentecost, this June 5, 1892.

Signed:

(Seal) JULIUS I, Archbishop of CEYLON, GOA, and the

INDIES.

Witnesses:

(Seal) W. MOREY, Consul of the United States at CEYLON,

(Seal) LISBOA PINTO F.E.A.D.M.S.

Rome, in accordance with its rules and customs, has never disputed the validity of Mgr. Vilatte.

In a letter from Mgr. Ceretti, Papal Nuncio, letter published by the "Courier of Bavaria," of Munich, and dated July 6, 1925, although published in issue 11 of the same month by this journal, it says this:

"Mgr. Vilatte has received the minor orders and the sub-deaconate on June 5, 1885, the diaconate on June 6 of the same year, and the priesthood on June 7, 1885. These different orders were conferred on him by Mgr. Herzog, 'Old Catholic' bishop, in the 'Old Catholic' Church of Berne. The documents which are proof of it bear the signature and the name of Mgr. Herzog.

"As regards his episcopal consecration, it took place on May 25, 1892. Mgr. Vilatte was consecrated by three Jacobite bishops in the Cathedral of archbishop Alvarez (Julius I), that is to say in the Our Lady of Good Death church, of Colombo, isle of Ceylon. Mgr. Vilatte is in possession of a bull of consecration signed by three bishops, and by the American consul who assisted at the ceremony." Signed: "Ceretti, Archbishop of Cerinth, and Papal Nuncio."

Here, therefore, is a recognition of the validity of Mgr. Vilatte which settles everything once and for all…

Now, it is here that it is necessary to remind oneself of this phrase by Pope Pious XI, concerning the book of N. Cabasilas: *Life in Jesus Christ*:

"Among the Catholics, they are sometimes lacking the just appreciation of their separated Brothers, because they do not know them. They do not know what there is precious, good, Christian, in these fractions of the Catholic truth. The blocks detached from the golden rock are themselves gold! ..."

And well before Pope Pious XI, the Church had already pronounced:

"The Holy Office estimates that the ordinations of the Jansenists and the Jacobites are valid."

Who said this? The Rev. Brother David Fleming, Consultor of the Holy Office, Definitor General of the Friars Minor in 1889.

The Rev. Brother William, Benedictine, had on the other hand published in a brochure entitled *The Genesis of the Old Catholic cult in America*, (Buffalo, 1898), another justification of the apostolic validity of this Jacobite filiation:

"The validity of the episcopal acts of Mgr. Mar Thimotheus (alias Mgr. Vilatte), has been recognized by Rome. A priest ordained by him is entered into the Roman Church, he is held to Rome. After an examination of the Sacred Congregation of the Rites, his ordination has been declared valid, and he has been allowed to celebrate under the altars of the Pope," (op. cit.).

Finally, the late Cardinal Richard, archbishop of Paris, in his letter of April 17, 1900, and the bishop of Evreux, in the "Semaine Religieuse" [Religious Week] of Evreux, from the same era, had protested against the ordinations made by the same Mgr. Vilatte at Paris, in 1900, and all while declaring them irregular, have nevertheless recognized that, "unfortunately, they would not be invalid…"

IV. TABLE OF THE APOSTOLIC SUCCESSION OF MGR. HOUSSAY

Saint Peter established his first apostolic see at Antioch in the Year 38, and since then, an uninterrupted succession of bishops have transmitted the powers of the apostle unto our day, (cf. Le Quien: Orienc Christianus, v. II, col. 1357-1408).

PATRIARCHS OF ANTIOCH

1. Saint Peter, apostle	38
2. Evodus	40
3. Ignatius I, martyr	43
4. Aaron	123
5. Cornelius	137
6. Eodos	142
7. Theophilus	157
8. Maximinus	171
9. Seraphim	179
10. Astlediaes (or Asclepiade), martyr	189
11. Philip	201
12. Sebinus	219
13. Babylos	237
14. Fabius	250
15. Demetrius	251
16. Paul I	259
17. Domnus I	270
18. Timotheus	281
19. Cyrilus	291
20. Tyrantus	296
21. Vitalius	301

PATRIARCHS OF ANTIOCH
(of the Jacobite lineage)

Jacob Baradai Zanzala having accomplished
the Jacobite reform, Sergius adopted his views
and became the 1st patriarch of this Church.

Restored in 616 the concord between the
Jacobite and Coptic sees.

   Constructed the 1st Church of Antioch
   with the authorization of the Caliph.
   Contracts in 726 the union with the
   Armenian at the Synod of Tofin.
   Composed a History of the Syrians and
   Passes his patriarchate in conflict with his
   adversaries.

Imprisoned at Constantinople after the
Capture of Antioch in 969 by the Greek
Emperor Nicephorus Phocas.

70. Athanasius IV	987
71. John VII	1004
72. Dionysius IV	1032
73. Theodorus II	1042
74. Athanasius V	1058
75. John VIII	1064
76. Basilius II	1074
77. Abdon	1076
78. Dionysius V	1077
79. Evanius III	1080
80. Dionysius VI	1088
81. Athanasius VI	1091
82. John IX	1131
83. Athanasius VII	1139
84. Michael I, the Great	1166

Transferred in 1166 the Jacobite patriarchate
to the town of Manlin (Turkey).

85. Athanasius VIII	1200
86. Michael II	1207
87. John X	1208
88. Ignatius III	1223
89. Dionysius III	1253
90. John XI	1253
91. Ignatius IV	1264
92. Philanus	1283
93. Ignatius Baruhid	1293

Starting from this patriarch, the name of
Ignatius is common to all his successors.

94. Ignatius Ismael	1333

95. Ignatius Basilius III	1366
96. Ignatius Abraham II	1382
97. Ignatius Basilius IV	1412
98. Ignatius Behanam I	1415
99. Ignatius Kalejih	1455
100. Ignatius John XII	1483
101. Ignatius Noah	1492
102. Ignatius Jesus I	1509
103. Ignatius Jacob I	1510
104. Ignatius David I	1519
105. Ignatius Abdullah I	1520
106. Ignatius Naamathalak	1557
107. Ignatius David II	1576
108. Ignatius Philathus	1591
109. Ignatius Abdullah II	1597
110. Ignatius Cadhai	1598
111. Ignatius Simeon	1640
112. Ignatius Jesus II	1653
113. Ignatius Messiah	1661
114. Ignatius Cabeed	1686
115. Ignatius Gervasius II	1687
116. Ignatius Isaac	1708
117. Ignatius Siccarablak	1722
118. Ignatius Gervasius III	1746
119. Ignatius Gervasius IV	1768
120. Ignatius Mathias	1781
121. Ignatius Behanam II	1810
122. Ignatius Jonas	1817
123. Ignatius Gervasius V	1818
124. Ignatius Elias II	1839
125. Ignatius Jacob II	1847
126. Ignatius Peter III	1872

Starting from this patriarch, the succession
is given by the episcopal consecrations
which follow, and the dates given are those
of the consecration.

127. Mgr. Paul Athanasius   1877
     Consecrated by H.B. Ignatius Peter III as
     Jacobite bishop.

128. Mgr. Julius I Alvarez, archbishop of Ceylon   1889
     By bull of December 29, 1891, dated in the
     monastery of Mardin, H.B. Ignatius
     Peter III, Jacobite Patriarch of Antioch,
     authorized Mgr. Alvarez to consecrate
     the priest Joseph-René Vilatte, while
     recognizing the latter by the title of
     archbishop.

129. Mgr. Joseph-René Vilatte   5/25/1892
     Consecrated in the Our Lady of Good
     Death cathedral at Colombo (Ceylon),
     founds the see of the Eglise Catholique
     Française (generally known under the
     name of Gallicane).

130. Mgr. Paolo Miraglia   5/6/1900
     Consecrated in the Church of
     Piacenza (Italy) as bishop of the
     Italian Catholic Church.

131. Mgr. Julien Houssay   12/4/1904
     Consecrated in the Old Catholic Church
     of Thiengen, duchy of Bade (Germany),
     archbishop of the Eglise Catholique
     Française.

V. THE DOCTRINE

"What is really *Catholic*, that is to say *universal*, is what has been believed and taught in all times, everywhere, and by all..." (St. Vincent de Lerins)

It has long been held that Abbé Julio, although come out of the Church of Rome and become, by the reception of the apostolic filiation, an authentic bishop, had nevertheless remained Catholic, in his teachings as in his episcopal behavior: liturgy, sacraments, etc.

We must first observe that there are here things absolutely distinct. The doctrine of a Church is one thing, its rites and their context are another.

We have said strongly that Mgr. Julien Houssay had become aware of the doctrine of Origen in the course of his stay at Pont-de-Ruan, in Touraine. We are now able then, in light of this finding, to specify the nature of the teachings that he had been led to communicate around him, since, as we know, they are those of Origen.

On the Creation.

God, Essential Being, Eternal, existing by Himself and in Himself, without needs and without variation, infinitely good, infinitely wise because infinitely perfect, is also all-powerful.

Being all-powerful and eternal, his omnipotence is then necessarily exercised for all eternity upon Creatures:

"The Lord has possessed me at the Beginning of His Course, before His most ancient Works..." (Proverbs VIII, 22).

"For I am going to create a new Heaven and a new Earth. And all that had been before, will be erased from memory, without which it will return to the spirit..." (Isaiah IXV, 17).

"For as the new Heavens and the new Earth that I am going to create will exist always before Me, says the Lord, so will your name and your race exist eternally... (Isaiah IXV, 23).

"My Father and I do not cease to act..." (John V, 17).

"Now therefore, my Father, glorify Me in Yourself, from that Glory that I have had in You before this world was..." (John XVII, 5).

Thus therefore, the Creations succeed Creations, the Universes succeed Universes, probably separated by periods of Non-Being, analogous to the famous "seventh day" during which "God rested," (Genesis II, 1).

When the Beings integrated in one of these Creations are freely manifested by their acts, by a sort of self-determination, when the end of this Creation occurs, they remain fixed in the final state that they have reached. And it is a sort of mysterious *Fire* that fixes them, hardens them, and tempers them, for the role that they have to play in the following Creation.

Thus, fixed in Evil, they will remain, in the new Creation, instruments of temptation, corruption, and destruction. These are the Demons.

Fixed in the Good, they remain in the new Creation instruments of liberation, purification, and creation. These are Angels, or Souls chosen and set apart, according to the happy expression of Paul:

"If the Lord of the hosts of Heaven had not

reserved for us any of our Race, we would have become like Sodom and Gomorrha…" (Romans IX, 29).

With regard to the Creatures not fixed, because they issued for the first time outside of Non-Being, the ones and the others will play their role, all while carrying within themselves their own hell or their own paradise, which state will endure as long as the Creation in which they participate.

The creations are called "ages" in the Scriptures. The Greek versions use the word "Aeons." They constitute cycles, several from among them constitute a general creation. This last is also called the "age of ages."

On the Preexistence of the Souls.

The word *Adam* does not designate a carnal being, but a collectivity. One says *Adam* as one says the *regiment*, or the *sailor*. The First Man was an egregore, a choir, and it is the central spirit of this choir who was the true Adam, the driving cell. In the words of Origen:

"The Souls are preexistent, as a sort of people…" The Scripture confirms this notion to us:

"It is not for you alone that I make this covenant and these execrations, but for all those who, *present before the Lord oar God, are not yet with us…*" (Deuteronomy XXIV, 14, 15).

"Before having formed you in the uterus, I have known you, and I have imposed Knowledge upon you. And before you came out of your mother's womb, I have sanctified you…" (Jeremiah I, 5).

"And I have praised the dead more abundantly

than the living, and I have judged *more favorably still, the one who has not yet been born*, and who has never seen the evils which have occurred under the sun..." (Ecclesiastes IV, 2, 3).

You are only *a single Body and a single Spirit*, just as you have only been called to a single hope..." (Ephesians IV, 4).

We must observe to the reader that in this brief study, we are not able to give to each of the paragraphs of the outline of the Origenist doctrine recovered by Abbé Julio, all the citations of Scripture which are related to it. We limit ourselves to the principal ones, to those which do not necessitate too considerable an esoteric development, which would weigh down the work.

We note, however, that most of the biblical citations related to the "Preexistence of the Souls" were often held as arguments in favor of the "Reincarnation of the Souls" by the advocates of the latter, the confusion being easy. We will return to this later on.

On Temptation and the Original Fall.

The notion of temptation (by the Principle of Evil and by the Beings that it has pulled along in its orbit), for the Preexistent Souls, was made an integral part of Judeo-Christianity. To deny that there has been a fall and spiritual degradation, is to deny the Incarnation of Christ; and to withdraw all value from the Redemption is equally to deny His Sacrifice. All this is unthinkable for a Christian.

One may therefore conceive of this Fall as the shattering of the egregore of which we spoke of previously, the dispersion of the collectivity, its *corruption*, analogous to that which follows corporeal death. And as it is a matter there of a fall caused by a spiritual degradation, this implies a descent into the planes of corresponding existence, that is to say the most inferior ones, by the effort of a progressive *materialization, leading towards animality*, and even beyond.

On the Redemption.

Just as a perverse Intelligence has darkened the preexisting Souls to the point of decay, so will it be a pure Intelligence that re-illuminates them.

"I have seen all the living men who walk under the sun, *and also the second Youth, which must rise in place of the Other*...N Ecclesiastes IV, 15).

We will not trouble the reader by recalling the very numerous verses of the Old Testament which speak of the Messiah, of his coming, and of the circumstances of it. Pages and pages would be necessary for this. The messianic prophecy is one of the most considerable (and also most striking) elements of the Scriptures.

An image will be better to grasp the process of Redemption.

If one imagines a necklace, one will observe that it is never called anything but "the necklace."

We break the thread. The pearls escape, falling to ground, falling in all directions. From then on, it is no longer a question of the necklace; one sets out to seek "the pearls."

Some of them are going to be lost under the

furniture, in obscure nooks. It will be necessary to wait a long time before they are found, despite the searches, and often by chance. Others will be quickly recovered, they will have never gone far from the point of the fall, nor from the vision of the owner of the necklace.

For these pearls bear within them, each, their own destiny, as the preexisting Souls bear in them theirs, by the effect of Predestination. And these pearls are, even them, submissive to their own destinies, enacted at the instant of their individual creation.

When the owner of the pearls will have recovered them, they will be threaded anew, on a new string, *in the initial order of their original placement, which was the function of their size and their water.* And when this reconstitution will be ended, one will speak again of the "necklace" and no longer of "the pearls."

If it lacks therein, the absence will be due to the imperfection of the means utilized for their search, or to the negligence of the seeker, or to the short duration of this search. But if our owner is *perfect*, if he *possesses all the means* necessary in order to seek the pearls, and if he has *all the time necessary* and no impatience, he will recover them all.

Replace the pearls with the Soul, the *necklace* with the Total Man, and the *owner* with God. Every problem of the final restitution is resolved, and the Apocatastasis is then justified.

On the Aposcatastasis or final Reintegration.

According to Origen, repeated by Abbé Julio, there is not an eternal hell. There are only abodes in a Creation; abodes corresponding to the ultimate state in which the Creature is found *fixed* at the time of the end of the Universe in which it has participated. It is therefore likewise, it seems, with paradise, which, with regard to this mode of reasoning, would be impermanent and transitory; the Creature being able, by its tepidity, to become unworthy and decay anew. In fact, this second point is not capable of being held back, the stage of *perfectibility* accessible to the Creature before permitting him, finally, to no longer be approachable by any temptation whatever. Furthermore, the period of self-determination of the being having ended, God, by an effect of his Grace no longer *leads him into temptation*, to paraphrase the prayer par excellence, the *Pater*. He takes away from the dark Entities every power over the Creature having finally ended his cycle of *probative manifestations*.

This final fixation of the *Good*, the Scriptures give us numerous witnesses:

"The Time ordained by Him being accomplished, they would all reunite in Jesus Christ as in the Head, as much in Heaven as on Earth…" (Ephesians I, 10).

"Children of Israel, you are with Me, says the Lord. But do not the children of Ethiopians belong to me also? I have taken Israel out of Egypt, but I have equally taken the Philistine's out of Cappadocia, and the Syrians from Cyrene…" (Amos IX, 7).

Abbé Julio is absolutely in the Origenian line of thought when we specify his thought on Hell. He admits strongly indeed the damnation of a being, but this "eternal death" is not the work of God, principle of all Life, but that of the being itself. Turning away *voluntarily* from God, the lost Creature falls under the yoke of the Prince of this World for such a duration that it may *give the idea of Eternity*, seeing as that it is a question, in fact, of the duration of the entire future Creation, this "age to come."

And thus the being, blinded and led astray, falls again into the midst of the churning of migrations. From life to life, falling each time a little farther below because of this progressive darkening, the lost Creature degrades each time a little more. In his *Livre Secret des Grands Exorcismes et Benedictions*, Abbé Julio tells us this on Hell:

"Hell is not a place, it is a state of being, the indefinite and vertiginous, above all *voluntary* descent, across all existence, into the somber night of Hatred, more dreadfully painful than all the senseless accounts of Hell, imagined by the wicked monks, in the aim of dominating and pressuring the ignorant masses.

"A ray of Hope, a sole act of Love.

"And the being, by one sole bond, may rise again to the Day. Satan *may* if he *wants*, become Lucifer again, but if he *does not want* it, he will suffer, just as all those who have imitated him, imitate him now, and will imitate him, the terrible, supreme, and final punishment, Eternal Death," (op. cit. page 503).

In regards to the tortures which would make the Abbé Julio smirk, we believe more real than he would suppose. If the damned, submitted anew to the law of transmigrations, descends from existence to existence, unto the *demoniacal* world of insects, *he will encounter there the very world of Cruelty*, of subtle, skillful, ingenious, refined cruelty. This entomology sets it before our eyes in a hallucinatory manner. Now, if a dream of a *few seconds* can allow us to unfold, upon the interior screen of our imagination, scenes and sensations which appear to us to last for a very long time, what does it say of the torture of so many unfortunate insects, knowingly paralyzed by the sting of so many others, *but never anesthetized*, and slowly devoured alive, over the course of long weeks, by the larva of their inspired executioner, or by itself?

In regards to Paradise, Abbé Julio reveals to us his thoughts, as a true gnostic: "Our conception of Paradise, that is to say the Life of the Beyond, is quite different. Studious men, we desire to understand better, to know more and more... *Outside of Knowledge, there is no struggle to live. Knowledge, therefore is Life.* This is the very conception of Christ, the Great Revealer, for whom it reflects well... " (op. cit. page 541).

Thus, therefore, for him Paradise is Knowledge, Gnosis.[4]

---

4. From the Greek gnosis, knowledge

On Reincarnation.

Like all the great doctors of Christianity, be it a question of those of the Eastern Church or of the Western Church, and those following, Abbé Julio was never a "reincarnationist." One would seek vainly indeed a passage of his works where he supports this theory, which we owe to Allan Kardec, under the classical form habitually propagated by his advocates[5].

Better yet, Abbé Julio has frequently combatted it in his writings. We will simply cite in this brief study this passage from his review "L'Entincelle," November 1902 issue, page 13, where he states this to us:

"Far from teaching reincarnation, Jesus and his Apostles, on the contrary, have taught the opposite…"

Without doubt, in his book *Les Grands Secrets Merveileux*, published in 1907, it tells us this on page 85, covering his biography written by Fabre des Essarts:

"We know that *u* is pronounced *ou* in German: we say Jean Houss, thus Houssay which is my name (Hous est). Moreover, moved by the Spirit I have gone to Constance. I have not recognized the hall of the Council, but I dreamt of my house and recognized the place of my torture.

---

5. It is only in the nineteenth century that it has thus appeared. Buddhism is absolutely unaware of it under this aspect, and Hinduism likewise. Islam rejects it, Judaism the same. And with regard to ancient Egypt, the religions of Chaldea, Babylon, and Assyria, one seeks there in vain! We possess in regards to this a dossier solidly stuffed! With regard to Pythagoreanism, it was only valid for the non-initiates, the profane. The initiates, by this very fact, would escape it. It was there the *aim of Initiation*.

I have relived all the phases."

This idea that he was the reincarnation of Jan Hus, because of Houssay, Abbé Julio owed to Fabre des Essarts and to the person who served him from time to time as a medium, who was fiercely reincarnationist. But Abbé Julio, if he supposed himself to have been Jan Hus, *absolutely did not make of reincarnation a general law*. He was too sincere a Christian and had made too good theological studies for this. The Telephone Directory includes several subscribers by the name of Napoleon, and this does not demonstrate that they are a reincarnation of this emperor. We must see in some of these lines the result of exterior pressures. But his thought, perfectly orthodox, has never varied upon this point in the course of the fourteen years of the publication of "L'Etincelle." He crossed too many courteous swords with his spirit friends, in the columns, for us to doubt it!

And in order to demonstrate that Reincarnation is a non-Christian teaching, he recalls to us in this same issue, this parable of Christ to his Apostles, that we find in the Gospel according to Saint Luke, that of poor Lazarus and the evil rich man, that we counsel strongly to the reader advocating reincarnation to read and re-read attentively, in chapter XVI, verses 19 to 31 of Luke. The framework of this brief study does not permit us to give it, considering its length. *But it gives us the formal teaching of Christ*, and it is by virtue of this that it is categorical in its teaching.

Another explanation, likewise from, Christ himself, on this subject, is also quite categorical. It is the account of the man blind from birth, cited in the Gospel of John, in chapter IX, verses 1 to 41. One blind from birth is presented to Christ. His disciples, wondering whether his infirmity *is the punishment for an evil action committed in a previous life*, or the expiation of a grave fault committed by his parents, ask him:

"Master, who has sinned, this man or his parents, that he was born blind?" And Jesus responded: "Neither he nor his parents have sinned... But it is so that the works of God be manifested in him..." And effectively, Jesus healed him, and later on the blind became one of his disciples.

The teaching of Christ is exposed by Paul in an absolutely clear manner in his *Epistle to the Hebrews*:

"For Jesus has not entered into this Sanctuary made by the hand of man (the temple of Jerusalem), and which had only prefigured the true on (Christ himself), he has entered into Heaven itself in order to present Himself henceforth on our behalf before the Face of God.

"And he has not entered there to offer Himself several times, like the high-priest of Israel entered all those years into the Sanctuary, while carrying the blood of a victim and not his own! For otherwise, it would have been necessary for Him to have suffered several times since the Creation of the World, instead of Him only appearing once at the end of the ages, in order to abolish Sin, by offering Himself as Victim.

"And this, as it is decreed that men die once, and are then judged..." (Hebrews IX, 25-27).

Here is cut short any possibility of a so-called "reincarnation" of Christ, as well as his Apostles. But another passage stresses again this impossibility:

"Thus Jesus Christ has been offered once, to erase the sins of all, and the second time, he will appear, having nothing more to do with sin, for the salvation of those who await him..." (Hebrews IX, 28).

Christ, by announcing *that he will return to His*

Father, has likewise many a time, done justice to this hypothesis.

Other passages of the Scriptures contradict or make impossible reincarnation. And here are some of them:

"Then Samuel said to Saul: 'Why have you troubled my rest by evoking me?...'" (I Kings, XXVIII, 15 or I Samuel XXVIII, 14 in the Protestant version).

"And here it was that two men conversed with Him (Jesus), and it was Moses and Elijah, who appeared surrounded by a sort of glory. They spoke of His departure, which would be accomplished at Jerusalem..." (Luke IX, 29-30).

Now, Moses died at the summit of mount Nebo, in the year 1451 before our era, and Elijah died in the year 1117 before Jesus Christ. There are, therefore, from fifteen to eleven centuries that the souls of these two prophets, as those of the Patriarchs, have been in "waiting." They are not, therefore, reincarnated. One will observe elsewhere that the "return of Elijah" which has been equated with John the Baptist, has no reference at all to the reincarnation of Elijah in John, for they must both return at the end of time. Which removes, obviously, the possibility that John is Elijah reincarnated!

The secret tradition of Christianity (which is less secret than commonly believed!), explains the words of Jesus in this way, declaring that John the Baptist is "already come..." A very high Angelic Entity has long ago rested upon Elijah the prophet. When his mission had ended, this Celestial Spirit had left Elijah, and it is he who is risen into Heaven in a "chariot of fire" (image of his subtle and incorruptible body). Later, the same Angelic Entity returned here below, and rested upon John the Baptist.

Thus one may say that the *true messenger* is already come. It will be by such an incorporation that two messengers, *identical* to Elijah and the Baptist, will manifest at the End of Time, to prepare the return of Christ in glory, like he did for his coming in the flesh.[6]

---

6. Abbé Julio obtained graces and supernatural healings by the intercession of the Saints. Which would be impossible if they reincarnated… In the words of Christ: The one who conquers, I will make a column in the Temple of My God, and he will come out of there no more…" (Apocalypse III, 12). But reincarnation is certainly a law for the non-Christians.

CONCLUSION

Thus, the humble Abbé Julio has properly received at the 131st degree, on December 4, 1904, by Mgr. Miraglia, in the Old Catholic Church of Thiengen (duchy of Bade), the succession of the Prince of the Apostles. Nothing is more incontestable.

At his death, occurring in Switzerland in 1912, he left nothing to his heirs, except some small debts. The religious life had not enriched him. The old fighter was able to make his own these words of Christ to his Apostles:

"Take neither gold, nor silver, nor change in your belts; nor sack for the journey, nor two tunics, nor shoes, nor staff, for the worker earns his food... You have received freely, give freely..." (Matthew X, 8-10).

But he left a greater wealth. That of his example, of his struggle for the Good, against Evil, and his inexhaustible charity. We wish for this Church of which he was the distant source (it will soon be a century since he was ordained priest, and soon sixty years since he became bishop) to dwell always in the path that he has thus traced, in advance, to his disciples:

"It is necessary to have *the gift*, which is not from one's will, but from the Spirit. It is necessary to develop this gift by the dignity of life, by faith, by prayer. One must seek neither glory, nor love of riches, nor hatred, nor vengeance, nor falsehood... One must never, under pain of downfall and the immediate loss of every gift, satisfy the vain curiosities, the base appetites, hidden grudges, irrational ambitions, and all the varied and limitless collections of human: folly, scarcely yet passed form the animal. It is necessary to have a heart burning with love for God and one's brothers..."

March 3, 1962, 118th anniversary of the birth of Abbé Julio: "Qui vicerit, possidebit hæc... " (Johan. Apoc. XXI, 7).

The 15 Most Powerful Prayers of Abbé Julio

DOMINE JESU CHRISTE
Luck at games

✠ Domine Jesu Christe, qui dixisti: Ego sum Via, Veritas et Vita: Ecce enim veritatem dilexisti, incerta et occulta sapientitæ tuæ manifestasti: mihi adhuc manifesta quæ revelet in hac nocte, sicut ita ravelatum ruit parvulis solis; incognita et ventura atque alia me doceas, ut possim omnia cognoscere, si sit et ita sit; monstra mihi mortem ornatam, omni cibo bono pulchrum et gratum pomarium, aut quamdam rem gratam; sin autem, ministra mihi ignem ardentem, aut fontem aquarum currentem, vel aliam quamcumaue rem quæ Domino placeant; et vel Angeli Ariel, Rubiel et Barachiel sitis mihi multum amatores et factores ad opus istud obtinendum…, quod ego N…, *(write first and last name)* cupio prævidere, cognoscere, scire, videre, habere et possidere, per illum Deum qui venturus est judicare vivos et mortuos et sæculum per ignem. Amen.

KYRIE CLEMENTISSIME
For a happy marriage

✠ Kyrie clementissime, qui Abraham servo tuo, dedisti uxorem Saram, et filio ejus obedientissimo, per admirabile signum, indicasti Rebeccam uxorem: indica mihi *(write first & last name)* servo tuo quam sim nupturus uxorem *(first & last name of the future bride)*, ancillæ tuæ quam sim nuptura virum *(first & last name of the future husband)*, per ministerium tuorum spirituum Michael, Raphael et Gabriel. Per Dominum nostrum Jesum Christum, qui vivit et regnat cum Deo Patre in unitate Spiritus Sancti, Deus, in sæcula sæculorum. Amen.

ELIAS ELOIM
For success, against every enemy

✠ Elias ✠ Eloim ✠ Eloa ✠ Leo ✠ Ya ✠ Eserchel ✠ Agla ✠ Sadai ✠ Adonai: Agios o Theos, Ischyros, Athanatos, eleison imas: Sanctus Deus, Fortis, Immortalis, adjuva me N…, famulum tuum (*or* famulam tuam) indignum (*or* indignam). Ab omni periculo, a morte æterna animæ et corporis, ab insidiis inimicorum, visibilium seu invisibilium eripe me.

✠ Jehovah ✠ Sabaoth ✠ Emmanuel ✠ Soter ✠ Tetragrammaton ✠ Omouzios ✠ Eheye ✠ Alpha et Omega ✠ Via, Veritas et Vita, mihi famulo tuo N… (*or* famulæ tuæ N…), salutaria sint altissima tua Nomina.

Dixisti: ✠ Hoc est corpus meum; dic: Me amet! et Amore tuo majus erit prodigium: Animæ conversio et salvatio: pessimas Potestates quæ contra me ruunt fortiter constringe.

In nomine ✠ Patris ✠ et Filii ✠ et Spiritus Sancti. Amen.

IMPARIBUS MERITIS
Against theft and thieves

Imparibus meritis pendent tria corpora ramis:
Dysmas et Gestas ✠ media est Divina Potesta;
Alta petit Dysmas, infelix intima Gestas:
Nos et res nostras conservet Summa Potestas;
Hos versus dicas ne te furto tua perdas.

PER CHRISTUM
Against sickness and evil

✠ Per Christum, et cum Christo, et in Christo, tibi Deo Patri omnipotenti, et in unitate Spiritus Sancti, laus honor et gloria. Per omnia sæcula sæculorum. Amen.

Oremus. Præceptis salutaribus moniti, et divina institutione formati, audemus dicere: *Pater noster, qui es in cælis*, etc.

Jesus! potentia Patria, sapientia Filii, virtus Spiritus Sancti, sanet hoc vulnus, depellat malum Istud… a me N… Amen.

Jesus! Domine Jesu Christe, credo quod nocte Jovis in Cœna, postquam lavasti pedes tuorum, accepisti panem sanctissimis manibus tuis, et benedixisti, et fregisti, et dedisti tuis Apostolis, dicens; Accipite et comedite: hoc est enim corpus meum; similiter accepisti calicem in sanctissimas manus tuas et gratias egisti, et tradidisti illis, dicens; Accipite et bibite, quia hie est meus sanguis novi testamenti, qui pro multis effundetur in remissionem peccatorum; hæc quotiescumque feceretis, facite in meam commemorationem. Obsecro te, mi Domine Jesu Christe, ut per hæc sanctissima verba et per virtutem illorum, et per meritum santissimæ Passionis tuæ sanetur hoc vulnus et malum istud. Amen.

Jesus! In nomine ✠ Patris ✠ et Filii ✠ et Spiritus Sancti. Amen.

IN NOMINE PATRIS
PRAYER OF DELIVERANCE
(from every possession, from temptation, from the evil
spirits, from obsession…)

✠ In nomine ✠ Patris ✠ et Filii ✠ et Spiritus
Sancti. Amen.

✠ Hel ✠ Heloym ✠ Soter ✠ Emmanuel ✠
Sabbaoth ✠ Agla ✠ Tetragrammaton ✠ Agios ✠ o Theos
✠ Ischyros ✠ Athanatos ✠ Jehovah ✠ Ya ✠ Adonai ✠
Sadai ✠ Omousios ✠ Messias ✠ Eserchel ✠ Increatus
Pater ✠ Increatus Filius ✠ Increatus Spiritus Sanctus ✠
Jesus ✠ Christus vincit ✠ Christus regnat ✠ Christus
imperat.

✠ Si Diabolus ligavit vel tentativit te N…, sua
effato vel per sua opera. Christus Filius Dei Vivi per suam
misericordiam liberet te ab omnibus spiritibus; immundis,
qui venit de Cœlo et incarnatus est in utero. Beatissimæ
Virginis Marim causa humanæ salutis, et ejiciendi diabolum
et omnem malignum a te in profundum inferni et abyssi.

✠ Ecce crucem Domini; ✠ fugite, partes adversæ,
✠ vicit leo de tribu, Juda, radix David. Alleluia!

*When one says this prayer, it is good to add to it the
Gospel of Saint John.*

ORISON OF SAINT CHARLEMAGNE
To be always protected

O God All-Powerful, who has suffered the death upon the gallows tree of the cross, to expiate all my sins, have mercy on me.

O Holy Cross of Jesus Christ, repel far away from me every sharp weapon.

O Holy Cross of Jesus Christ, preserve me from every corporeal accident.

O Holy Cross of Jesus Christ, pour out upon me every good.

O Holy Cross of Jesus Christ, turn away from me every evil, see that I am able to save my soul.

O Holy Cross of Jesus Christ, remove from me all fear of death, and grant me eternal life.

O Holy Cross of Jesus Christ, keep me, and see that the malign Spirits, whether visible or invisible, flee before me, from today and unto all the ages of ages. So mote it be!

It is also true that Jesus is born this day of Noel, also true that Jesus has been circumcised, also true that Jesus has received the offerings from the three Magi Kings, also true that Jesus has been crucified on Good Friday, also true that Joseph and Nicodemus have removed Jesus from the Cross and have placed him in the sepulchre, also true that Jesus is resurrected and ascended to heaven; just as it is also true that Jesus preserves me and will preserve me from every assassination attempt of my enemies, whether visible or invisible, from today and unto all the ages of ages. So mote it be.

O God All-Powerful, under the protection of ✠ Jesus, Mary, Joachim; ✠ Jesus, Mary, Anna; ✠ Jesus, Mary, Joseph; I place myself in your hands. So mote it be.

O Lord, by the bitterness that you have suffered for me upon the Holy Cros, principally when your soul is separated from its body, have mercy on my soul when it will be separated from this world. So mote it be!

FORMULA OF HEALING

When it is a matter of healing wounds or any sickness, those who have a great confidence in the power of the Name of Jesus and in the intercession of his humble servant Jean Sempé, are able, as he did himself during his mortal life, to make the signs of the cross upon the joints, or upon the wounds, or from head to foot, according to the type of illness.

At the same time one makes the signs of the cross, one will pronounce after the special Prayers, in all cases, the following formula:

✠ In the name of Jesus, cease to make him (her, me) suffer.

✠ In the name of Jesus, I will it and I command you: Leave, return to whence you came and remain there forever.

In the name of the ✠ Father, ✠ and of the Son, ✠ and of the Holy Spirit. So mote it be.

✠ Evil, whatever you be, from wherever you come, whatever be your nature or your origin, I order you in the Name of Jesus, which all obey in the heavens, upon the earth and unto the infernal regions, to leave N... this creature of God here present. I order you, in the Name ✠ of the Father, ✠ and of the Son, ✠ and of the Holy Spirit. So mote it be.

DESPERATE AFFAIRS
Litany of Saint Jude

Lord, have mercy on me.

Jesus Christ, have mercy on me.

Lord, have mercy on me.

Jesus Christ, hear me.

Jesus Christ, answer me.

Heavenly Father, who art God, have mercy on me.

God the Son, redeemer of the world, have mercy on me. God the Holy Spirit, have mercy on me.

Holy Trinity, who art one sole God, have mercy on me.

Saint Mary, queen of the apostles, pray for me.

Saint Joseph, patron of the Universal Church, pray for me.

Saint Peter, first of the apostles, pray for me.

Saint Jude, relative of Jesus and Mary, pray for me.

Saint Jude, who has been worthy to see Jesus and Mary and to enjoy their sweet conversations, pray for me.

Saint Jude, who has left all to follow Jesus, pray for me.

Saint Jude, who has persevered with Jesus in the midst of his persecutions, pray for me.

Saint Jude, who has had the honor to see your divine Master lower himself to wash your feet, pray for me.

Saint Jude, who at the Last Supper has been fed from the Body of Jesus Christ, pray for me.

Saint Jude, who has suffered so during the Passion of your divine Master, pray for me.

Saint Jude, who has been ravished with joy at the sight of Jesus resurrected, pray for me.

Saint Jude, who has seen Jesus ascend into heaven, pray for me.

Saint Jude, who has been filled with the Holy Spirit on the day of Pentecost, pray for me.

Saint Jude, who has preached valiantly in Jerusalem the resurrection of Jesus Christ, pray for me.

Saint Jude, who has converted innumerable people to the faith, pray for me.

Saint Jude, who has operated brilliant marvels by the virtue of the Holy Spirit, pray for me.

Saint Jude, who has given life to the soul and body of an idolatrous king, pray for me.

Saint Jude, who has imposed silence on the demon and confounded its oracles, pray for me.

Saint Jude, whose words, like arrows, pierce the hearts of those who would hear, pray for me.

Saint Jude, who, scorning the threats of the impious, has fearlessly preached the religion of Jesus Christ, pray for me.

Saint Jude, who has had the good fortune to die under the axe of the executioner for the glory of your divine Master, pray for me.

Saint Jude, who is ever seated at the table of the King of kings, pray for me. Saint Jude, who must one day judge the tribes of Israel, pray for me.

Saint Jude, that the faithful call the Patron of Desperate Causes, and who shows by your intercession that you enjoy a great prestige near to God, pray for me.

See, O Saint Jude, that the Church of Jesus Christ be more and more exalted; we pray to you, hear us.

See, O Saint Jude, that the souls of the true believers strengthen themselves in faith day in and day out, we pray to you, hear us.

See, O Saint Jude, that the regions of old evangelized by you remain Christian; we pray to you, hear us.

See, O Saint Jude, that God sends Apostles to all the peoples seated in the shadow of death; we pray to you, hear us.

See, O Saint Jude, that the people who have received the gift of faith never have the misfortune of losing it; we pray to you, hear us.

See, O Saint Jude, that the teaching of the Christian truth be given to all children; we pray to you, hear us.

See, O Saint Jude, that the persecutions of the Church cease and that the Kingdom of God comes upon the earth; we pray to you, hear us.

See, O Saint Jude, that all those who would invoke you in their necessity find themselves consoled and strengthened; we pray to you, hear us.

See, O Saint Jude, that all those who would invoke you upon the earth one day enjoy the eternal beatitude, we pray to you, hear us.

Lamb of God, who takes away the sins of the world, we pray to you, hear us.

Lamb of God, who takes away the sins of the world, we pray to you, hear us.

Lamb of God, who takes away the sins of the world, we pray to you, hear us.

V/. Pray for us, blessed holy Apostle Jude.

R/. So that we may become worthy of the

promises of Jesus Christ.

Let us pray. Glorious Apostle, martyr and relative of Jesus, Saint Jude, who has spread the faith among the most barbarous and remote nations; who has produced to Jesus innumerable people by the virtue of the holy word; see, I beseech you, that from the day I renounce sin and the occasions to sin, that I be preserved from every evil thought, and that I obtain always your relief in the most desperate causes.

As your heart is specially placed to come to the aid of the afflicted souls, I have confidence that you will think of me with sentiments of a tender mercy. Encouraged by the grand graces that you are accustomed to obtaining for the most troubled souls, I dare to make known to you this or that spiritual or temporal need. I dare to ask you to give to my poor heart this or that consolation.

The name of the traitor Judas who delivered your Master makes you forgotten by a very great number of Christians. But the true Church invokes you everywhere as the patron of desperate causes. Pray for me; deliver me from my pains; so that being more free to serve God in this life, I may be able one day to be admitted to the eternal joys with you and all the elect. So mote it be.

PRAYER AGAINST EVERY SICKNESS

Lord, the one that you love is sick. I dare to ask of you that his sickness be not at all to death, but that it serves to your glory and his sanctification. I believe that you are Christ, the Son of the Living God, who is come into the world. I believe that you are the resurrection and the life, that the one who believes in you will live, though he be dead; and that all those who live and who believe in you will never die. I believe, Lord; support my little faith. You have healed so many sick, during the time of your mortal life, at the prayer and consideration of those who would present themselves to you! I am not worthy to present myself before you, and I do not deserve that you should consider my prayer. I know that the children's bread ought never to be thrown to the dogs; but the little dogs eat the crumbs that fall from the table of their masters. If you will it, you are able to heal him; say a word, and he will be healed. Let this corporeal sickness serve to the healing of his soul and to our instruction. Give him patience, and to us charity. Hear him in the day of his affliction, save him, and give us the joy to praise you yet here below with him in your Holy Temple, and to bless you always in heaven. So mote it be!

My Father, remove from me this chalice; however, let your will be done and not mine.

Lord, do not put me back into your fury, and do not punish me in your anger. Have mercy on me, because I am weak; heal me because my bones are troubled.

There are neither remedies nor medicines that may be applied that give healing; it is your omnipotent word, O Lord; heal me and I shall be saved.

Lord, I suffer a violent pain; give to my prayer a favorable response.

I pass again before you all the years of my life in the bitterness of my heart.

I fear to die, because I am not at all yet prepared.

Remember me, Lord; do not avenge my sins, and do not remember my faults.

My God, I abandon myself to your mercy: use it in my regard.

Jesus, Son of David, have mercy on me; come to me before I die.

To my relief, great God! For I perish without you; but if I must die: your Heaven, give it to me!

Do not forget to carry upon oneself and to recite for nine days the prayer upon parchment, Per Christum.

THE GRAND UNIVERSAL PRAYER

✠ Spiritual fluids of Christ, come to me, come to us!

Spiritual fluids of all my brothers, unite with mine to those of Jesus Christ, and concentrate us all in Him!

Spiritual fluids of all men living and dead, incarnate and discarnate, establish yourselves in the harmonious communion of souls, of which Christ is the organic center.

Sacred aromas, living spirits of the adorable blood of Jesus Christ, enter into circulation among all the members of Humanity, so that this Humanity may become all the sooner the social Body of Christ.

Divine leaven, whose living hearth is in the heart of Jesus, regenerate us, vivify us, sanctify us.

Absolutely pure essence, which, by the Incarnation of the Word, you are inoculated against the fallen nature and have retaken possession of humanity to reintegrate it into the primordial conditions of its original holiness, rekindle in us the celestial spark, resuscitate in our hearts the divine principle which is dormant, paralyzed and as good as dead in the flesh and blood, and increase us *unto the heights of the fullness of Christ*, to the *new man*, which must take the place in each of us of the old man. Help our personal words to identify themselves with the divine *Word*.

Inhabitants of the celestial Carmel, come to the relief of our unfortunate brethren who detached themselves from you originally, and who, fallen from the *spiritual pole*, where you have remained in your glorious state, have come to run aground at the *material Pole* of creation. Help us, through your suggestions and your Redemption, and facilitate in us the means to conform us to love, in order to hasten the total accomplishment.

Cosmogonic Powers, living and intelligent Forces of nature, *spiritual Volitions*, Dynamic rectors of the spheres, that we call the Laws of the Universe, superior Spirits, who govern the worlds and direct the people; Blessed Archangel Michael, glorious Genius, who presides over the destined of the Fatherland; and you, Protectors of Paris and of France, Saint Genevieve, Saint Catherine, Saint Marguerite, Joan of Arc, Saint Louis; Patrons of all the diocese and all the parishes of France and of Christianity; Guardian Angels of all the French and of all men, assist us in the acute crisis that we are going through at this moment and which is on the verge of success.

Eternal Principle of life, Creator of Heaven and Earth, Father-Mother of all beings, great and small, visible and invisible, I adore you in Jesus Christ, through Jesus Christ and with Jesus Christ. We beseech you to apply to us without delay the blessing of the fruit of the general redemption. It is done, since you have loved the world to the point of giving your only Son, O my God! It is done, since Christ has taken upon himself all our iniquities to expiate them in his blood and to reconcile us with you: apply to us, therefore, these merits, good, just and merciful Father, for by ourselves, as you well know, O my God, we are incapable of appropriating them for ourselves.

The harvest is ready, as has said the Messiah, it is abundant. Who lacks it are the workers who must gather it. O Lord who art the Master of this harvest, send at the soonest your harvesters, your new Apostles, your new

Evangelists and your new Missionaries. Come through them, Lord, without delay. Excite your power, your mercy and your charity. Without you we can do nothing at all. In you alone, is the Salvation, the Resurrection and the Life.

All strength, all efficacy, all grace, all light, and every perfect gift descends from you. Open at last upon the earth the era of great pardon and great mercy; inaugurate the *Universal Jubilee*, to which all the Jubilees of the old and new Law were only preludes and prophetic announcements. Proclaim Amnesty, Justice, Peace and Happiness for all.

O you who, in saving us, has saved us freely, save us, source of piety. There is no one who can fight for us, unless it is you Lord, our God.

We beseech you, Lord, to throw a glance upon this family, who is Yours and for which Our Lord Jesus Christ has not hesitated to deliver himself into the hands of the impious and to submit to the torture of the cross, he who lives and reigns with you unto the ages of ages.

So mote it be! So mote it be! So mote it be!

PRAYER OF SAINT CYPRIEN
To bind and expel the malign spirit

✠ I, N…, servant of O.L.J.C., have prayed to the Father All-Powerful and have said to him:

You alone are the Strong God, O God All-Powerful, who inhabits the heavens, abode filled with light. You alone are holy and worthy of praise, and you have foreseen from all eternity the malice of your servant and the iniquities into which I was plunged by the power of the demon. But I ignored your Holy Name, I walked in the midst of the sheep, and they left me at once; the storm clouds were no longer able to give rain upon the earth, which was dry and arid; the trees were no longer able to give their fruits, neither were the women pregnant, who endured intolerable suffering; the passages of the sea were closed, and it was impossible to reopen them. It is I myself who was the cause of all these evils and an infinity of others. But now, my Lord Jesus Christ and my God, that I make known your Holy Name and that I may love it, I repent with all my heart, with all my soul and with all my strength, of the multitude of my malices, of my iniquities and of my crimes, and I make the resolution to dwell in your love and submit myself to your holy commandments, because you are the one and only Word of the Father All-Powerful. I conjure you now, my God, to lead and to reunite the sheep to the same pasture; and break the bonds of the storm clouds and make to fall upon the earth and upon your children the little rains, gentle and favorable, which produce food for man as well as the animals; to give a successful fertility to the entirety of nature, from the vegetable up to the intellectual being; to unbind the rivers and the seas that my faults have bound as well as all the rest.

Preserve me N…, who has the good fortune to belong to you, being your creature, ✠ from all peril, ✠ from all danger, ✠ and from all evil. I ask it of you and entreat of you, O my God, by your Most Holy Name, to which all things, whether spiritual or corporeal, ought to give honor and glory; by Emmanuel, which means God with us, who said to the waters: I have sanctified the gates through which you pass; by your servants Moses and Aaron, I entreat of you, O you, Lord, who formerly has delivered the children of Israel from the captivity of Pharaoh, extend upon me, N…, your right hand and your holy blessing.

You are my God; bless me, as you have blessed your Angels, Archangels, Thrones, Dominions, Principalities, Powers, Virtues, Cherubim and Seraphim. Deign also, my Lord Jesus Christ, to bless me, N…, your creature, bless me in such fashion that no impure Spirit, nor Demon is able to harm me; may I not be able to receive any blemish; may neither their evil designs, nor their malicious actions, nor the malignity of their eyes and their poisoned tongues, nor any persecution on their part be able to have any touch upon me. Remove from me, Lord, every evil and every malign Spirit. All your enemies and adversaries are mine, all the evil men and pernicious women, may N… and N… be removed from me and I far from them; may they flee me and not have any influence nor power over me. I ask this of you by the virtue of the Most High. And if someone, Lord, wishes to harm or do the slightest evil to me, place me under your holy protection, me N..., your servant, and deign to do all good for me. I ask this of you by the virtues and the merits of your holy Angels, who praise you ceaselessly, O my God, and by all your Patriarchs, your Apostles, your Saints in Paradise, to deliver and preserve N..., your servant, from the malignity of the looks of all my enemies and from all those who may be able to harm me. So mote it be.

I pray you once more, my Lord Jesus Christ, by all the holy prayers which are spoken in all the churches by the Christian, to set me free and deliver me from the malignity of all evil actions, from all evil spells, that are able to set the demons, the evil men and women, and particularly N... and N... against me N... your creature whom you love. I ask this of you by the name of Cherubim and Seraphim, may they have not any power nor influence over me. I beseech you most humbly, O Jesus most gentle and merciful, by your Annunciation, by your Passion, by your death, by your burial, by your admirable resurrection, by your marvelous Ascension, by the coming of the Holy Spirit upon the earth, by the beauty of Adam, by the innocence of Abel, by the deliverance of Noah, by the faith of Abraham, by the obedience of Isaac, by the gentleness of Jacob, by the religion of Melchizidek, by the patience of Job, by the power of Moses, by the holiness of Aaron, by the victory of Joshua, by the Psalms of David, by the wisdom of Solomon, by the tears of Jeremy, by the strength of Samson, by the contrition of Zachariah, by the baptism of John the Baptist, by the voice of the Celestial Father speaking from on high from his throne and which the world heard: this one is my beloved Son, in whom I have placed all my kindness, listen to him; by this great miracle, by which Jesus satiated five thousand people in the desert with Lazarus, by the one who performs it again each day in giving himself really to us in the Eucharist; by the primacy of Peter, by the knowledge of Paul, by the purity of John, by the preaching of the Apostles, by the words of the Evangelists, by the prayers of all the Saints; by the height of the heavens, by the depths of the infernal abyss, by the enlightenment of Divinity, by all those who fear God: I beseech you, Lord, to break all these bonds that wish to hem me in and preserve me from all the charms, enchantments, spells and other traps that wish to set N… and N… against me N…, who am the servant of God.

I conjure you, Lord, by all these holy actions and by all the virtues which are written in this book to the praise and honor of the Great Living God, that these charms have not any influence over me N… your servant. may this Great God, who has created all things, not allow that any of their magic, witchcraft or evil spells, whether they or those that serve them, have any power over the gold, silver, the bronze, the iron; upon all that is embroidered, chiseled or raw; upon the silk, upon the wool, upon the linen and upon the threads of cloths made of some other material; upon all the bones, whether from man or woman and of any species of animal; upon the wood or upon whatever other material it may be, upon the herbs, upon the books, inscribed papers or virgin parchment, whether they place there in or cause it to be placed upon any stone, in the water, sepulchre of some dead, be they Jew, pagan or Christian; in or upon the hair, the clothes, the shoes, cords or belts; in a word, in or upon anything that may exist, that is to say in any place or thing that all these evil actions be made or are able to be made. I ask you and pray you most humbly by the virtue ✠ of God the Father All-Powerful, ✠ and of the Son Redeemer, ✠ and of the Holy Spirit Vivifier, to destroy them and render them useless, and may they not have any power over me ✠ N…, who am your servant. So mote it be!

✠ I conjure you thereof by the merits of St. Cyprian.

In the name ✠ of the Father, ✠ and of the Son, ✠ and of the Holy Spirit. So mote it be.

PRAYER TO SAINT ANTHONY OF PADOUA

To find a person or recover an object
(said for nine days)

✠ Great Saint, Anthony of Padoua, luminous flame, I pray you to enlighten my spirit, so that I am able to find...; see that I outwit the ruses of Satan and that I emerge victorious from the traps that he lays for me to ruin me and afflict me. I beseech you by the knowledge that the Holy Spirit has so greatly shed in your soul to enlighten the Universe. Obtain for me also an active faith, a perfect receptiveness to the inspiration of grace, a disgust for the vain pleasures of the world and an ardent desire for the ineffable joys of eternal blessedness. So mote it be!

PRAYER TO DEFEND ONESELF FROM EVERY KNOWN ENEMY

Archangel Michael, guardian of Paradise, come to relieve the people of God, may it be agreeable to you to defend against the demon, and generally against our enemies who are very powerful, and finally to lead us into the presence of God to the place of blessedness.

Lord my God I will give my most humble homage in your holy temple, and I will publicize the greatness of your Name.

I will sing your praises in the presence of your Angels.

Now, Jesus passing among them, went…

✠ May Jesus, Our Lord, be blessed now and always. As he is our Savior, he will lead us happily unto the path he has marked.

✠ Jesus, may the darkness blind our enemies, without which they are able to have use of their eyes, and as a mark of their unworthiness, may they be stooped towards the ground.

✠ Jesus, shed upon them the effect of your indignation, and may your just anger give them continual alarm; may horror and fright bring down their courage, at the sole idea of your strength.

✠ Jesus, see that they become immobile like stones, until that I, N…, who am your creature, that you have redeemed by your precious blood, be past.

✠ Jesus, the strength of your arms is always outstanding; by this same strength, exterminate the powerful enemies, in bringing low the arrogance of these impious ones raised against me.

✠ Jesus, keep me from those who rise up from all sides in the design to ruin me.

✠ Jesus, save me from the hand of the wicked and pull me away from this unjust man (or woman).

✠ Jesus, deliver me from those who commit evil, who seek to spill my blood or who desire my life, my honor and my belongings.

✠ God is my guard and my defense against all sorts of beasts unchained against me; his hand will serve as my shield against the arrows of my enemies. I am without fear, when I will see a hundred-thousand at my sides; God has placed his arms about me, and I will not know how to get lost or stray under his guidance.

✠ Glory to the Father, to the Son, to the Holy Spirit, from the beginning and unto all eternity, today and always, unto all the ages of ages, So mote it be!

PSALMS 51 & 139
AGAINST SLANDERERS & SCANDAL-MONGERERS

The evils caused by an evil tongue have done more ravages than ten plagues and thirty battles.

Psalm 51

Why boastest thou thyself in mischief, O mighty man? the goodness of God endureth continually.

Thy tongue deviseth mischiefs; like a sharp razor, working deceitfully.

Thou lovest evil more than good; and lying rather than to speak righteousness. Selah.

The righteous also shall see, and fear, and shall laugh at him:

Lo, this is the man that made not God his strength; but trusted in the abundance of his riches, and strengthened himself in his wickedness.

But I am like a green olive tree in the house of God: I trust in the mercy of God for ever and ever.

I will praise thee for ever, because thou hast done it: and I will wait on thy name; for it is good before thy saints.

Psalm 139

Deliver me, O LORD, from the evil man; preserve me from the violent man;

Which imagine mischiefs in their heart; continually

are they gathered together for war.

They have sharpened their tongues like a serpent; adders' poison is under their lips. Selah.

Keep me, O LORD, from the hands of the wicked; preserve me from the violent man; who have purposed to overthrow my goings.

The proud have hid a snare for me, and cords; they have spread a net by the wayside; they have set gins for me. Selah.

I said unto the LORD, Thou art my God: hear the voice of my supplications. O LORD.

O GOD the Lord, the strength of my salvation, thou hast covered my head in the day of battle.

Grant not, O LORD, the desires of the wicked: further not his wicked device; lest they exalt themselves. Selah.

As for the head of those that compass me about, let the mischief of their own lips cover them.

Let burning coals fall upon them: let them be cast into the fire; into deep pits, that they rise not up again.

Let not an evil speaker be established in the earth; evil shall hunt the violent man to overthrow him.

I know that the LORD will maintain the cause of the afflicted, and the right of the poor.

Surely the righteous shall give thanks unto thy name: the upright shall dwell in thy presence.

www.ingramcontent.com/pod-product-compliance
Lightning Source LLC
La Vergne TN
LVHW090047090426
835511LV00031B/481